The Servant King
Mark 9–16

Series Editor: Tim Chester

GoodBook COMPANY

The Servant King
Mark 2: a good book guide
© Tim Chester/The Good Book Company, 2006

The Good Book Company
Tel: 0845-225-0880
Fax: 0845-225-0990
Email: admin@thegoodbook.co.uk
Internet: www.thegoodbook.co.uk

Unless indicated, all Scripture references are taken from the HOLY BIBLE,
NEW INTERNATIONAL VERSION. Copyright © 1973, 1978, 1984 International Bible
Society. Used by permission.

ISBN: 1 904889 51 4
ISBN 13: 9781904889519

Printed in the UK

CONTENTS

Introduction: Good Book Guides

Every Bible-study group is different—yours may take place in a church building, in a home, in a cafe, on a train, over a leisurely mid-morning coffee or squashed into a 30-minute lunch break. Your group may include new Christians, mature Christians, non-Christians, mums and tots, students, businessmen or teens. That's why we've designed these *Good Book Guides* to be flexible for use in many different situations.

Our aim in each session is to uncover the meaning of a passage, and see how it fits into the 'big picture' of the Bible. But that can never be the end. We also need to appropriately apply what we have discovered to our lives. Let's take a look at what is included:

⊕ **Talkabout:** most groups need to 'break the ice' at the beginning of a session, and here's the question that will do that. It's designed to get people talking around a subject that will be covered in the course of the Bible study.

⊕ **Investigate:** the Bible text for each session is broken up into manageable chunks, with questions that aim to help you understand what the passage is about. **The Leader's Guide** contains **guidance on questions**, and ☑ additional 'follow-up' questions.

⊡ **Explore more (optional):** these questions will help you connect what you have learned to other parts of the Bible, so you can begin to fit it all together like a jig-saw.

⊡ **Apply:** As you go through a Bible study, you'll keep coming across **apply** sections. The first part has questions to get the group discussing what the Bible teaching means in practice for you and your church. The second part, ⊡ **getting personal**, is an opportunity for you to think, plan and pray about the changes that you personally may need to make as a result of what you have learned.

⊡ **Pray:** We want to encourage prayer that is rooted in God's Word—in line with His concerns, purposes and promises. So each session ends with an opportunity to review the truths and challenges highlighted by the Bible study, and turn them into prayers of request and thanksgiving.

The **Leader's Guide** and introduction provide historical background information, explanations of the Bible texts for each session, ideas for **optional extra** activities, and guidance on how best to help people uncover the truths of God's Word.

Why study Mark 9-16?

*For even the Son of Man did not come to be served, but to serve,
and to give his life as a ransom for many.*
Mark 10 v 45

Expectations can be a problem—if they're wrong! Have you ever arranged to meet someone for the first time, only to miss them because you expected someone who looked quite different? Later perhaps, you had a good laugh about it… but how devastating to miss God Himself, just because you expected *Him* to look different…

In first-century Israel, people had completely wrong expectations about the Messiah—God's promised King, sent to rescue Israel. When they saw Jesus they refused to believe in Him. How could God's King come to serve and suffer? How could Israel's Messiah judge Israel's leaders and their precious temple? How could the promised Rescuer not rescue Himself from the cross? Because of their wrong expectations they rejected Him.

But in Mark's Gospel chapters 1–8, the very ordinary disciples of Jesus had already come to see, with the 'eyes of faith', that this carpenter turned travelling teacher was, in fact, God's King, Judge and Son. Chapters 9–16 go on to show us what it means to follow this very different Servant King. It means denying yourself, taking up your cross, losing your own life, and trusting instead in Jesus' promise of eternal life in the age to come. It means praying daily: 'I do believe; help me overcome my unbelief!'

Do Christians today make the same mistake as those in Jesus' day? Perhaps you are a new believer looking forward to a new life of following Jesus and expecting everything to be wonderful. Perhaps you have been a Christian for years, and you wonder why the Christian life is such a struggle. Surely, if God was truly with His people, things wouldn't be like this! Or perhaps you are still investigating things, and want to discover what authentic Christianity really is.

Too often our ideas of 'blessing' or 'success' are shaped by the false values of the world, not God—by what we see, rather than by faith. The second half of Mark is packed with challenges and encouragement to help us live by faith, not by sight, and this *Good Book Guide* will help us learn what it really means to follow our Servant King.

1

Mark 8 v 31 – 9 v 50
THE EXAMPLE OF THE KING

⊕ talkabout

1. Think about the way in which most people picture 'success'. As a group, come up with a popular description of a 'successful' person. By contrast, how do you think Christians would describe a successful person?

The first half of Mark's Gospel asks the question: 'Who is this?' (4 v 41). It comes to a climax when Peter answers the question by confessing that Jesus is the Christ—God's promised Saviour King (8 v 29). Jesus warns the disciples not to tell people this (8 v 30). The reason is that the disciples do not yet understand what it means for Jesus to be the Christ. They are expecting the promised Christ to come in triumph and glory.

⊕ investigate

▶ Read Mark 8 v 31-38

2. Explain from these verses what it means for Jesus to be God's promised Saviour King.

3. Why do you think Peter rebukes Jesus?

4. Why does Jesus call Peter 'Satan'?

5. What does Jesus say following Him will involve?

6. What wonderful promise is given to those who follow Jesus?

⤳ apply

7. In what ways are we tempted to be ashamed of Jesus and His words (8 v 38)? Give specific examples.

• How do you think Jesus would define 'success'? Compare your answers with those discussed in Question 1.

⊡ getting personal

What kind of success are you aiming for? In which areas of life do you need to repent of seeking the wrong kind of success, and follow Jesus' words instead?

⊥ investigate

Chapters 9-10 describe the journey of Jesus, and His disciples, to Jerusalem. This is the way to the cross. In these chapters Jesus explains what it means to be His disciple. This teaching is built around three predictions of His death (8 v 31; 9 v 31; 10 v 32-34). We learn that to follow Jesus is to accept the way of the cross—a life of service and sacrifice.

❯ Read Mark 9 v 2-13

8. We might expect the voice from heaven to say: 'Look how amazing and glorious He is'. What does it say instead? Why?

❯ Read Mark 9 v 14-29

9. This section raises the question: 'How can Jesus' followers cope when He is gone?' What is the problem affecting Jesus' disciples and what answer is given in these verses?

10. Look at 9 v 29. What is the 'prayer' that is offered to Jesus in this story? How does this help us understand 9 v 29?

❯ Read Mark 9 v 30-50

11. In verses 30-32 Jesus again predicts His death. What practical lessons for His followers does Jesus draw out from the pattern of service and sacrifice that will be shown in His crucifixion (see verses 33-50)?

➡ apply

12. What can we learn about ourselves from the disciples' failures?

• And what can we do practically to ensure that we 'listen to Him'?

🔅 getting personal

Do you see in yourself the same weaknesses as the disciples—failing to listen to Jesus' words or trust Him to do what you cannot? Or have you become complacent about following Him, confident in your own abilities instead? What changes do you need to pray about and plan for?

⬆ pray

Think about God...
• Think of all the reasons why you can give praise and thanks to God that Jesus came as a Servant, not as a conqueror

Think about yourself...
• In which areas of your life is the prayer of 9 v 24 relevant for you?

Think about others...
• Who do you know who is struggling with unbelief, or has failed to truly understand the words of Jesus? What about those who do understand, but are ashamed of Jesus' words? How can you pray for them?

2 Mark 10
THE WAY OF THE KING

⊕ ## talkabout

1. With a partner, make a list of some of the ways in which people today 'want everything now.' Can you think of how this influences us to make wrong decisions?

Mark chapters 9-10 are about what it means to follow Jesus. Three times Jesus predicts His death (8 v 31; 9 v 31 and 10 v 32-34). To be a disciple is to accept the way of service and sacrifice modelled by Jesus in the cross. Jesus promises that those who follow Him will save their lives, but first they must deny themselves and give their lives to His service.

⊥ ## investigate

▶ **Read Mark 10 v 1-12**

The Pharisees test Jesus by trying to get Him caught in a debate. Some Jews in Jesus' day thought divorce was only permissible for adultery. Others thought men could divorce their wives virtually at will.

2. Look at verses 2-5. What is the point that Jesus is making?

3. Look at verses 6-9. What is God's purpose for human sexuality?

4. How does this teaching on divorce fit in with what Jesus is saying about the way of the cross?

explore more

What grounds does the Bible give for divorce? **See Matthew 5 v 32 and 19 v 8-9; also 1 Corinthians 7 v 12-15**. Why do you think these exceptions are not mentioned in the teaching of Jesus recorded by Mark in 10 v 10-12?

investigate

> **Read Mark 10 v 13-31**

5. What does Jesus reveal about God in verses 13-16?

6. What does it mean to receive the kingdom of God like a child?

7. Why do you think Mark puts the story of the children next to the story of the rich young ruler?

8. How does the young man illustrate what Jesus said in 8 v 34-37?

9. Look at verses 29-31. How do Christians receive 'a hundred times as much in this present age'?

⤳ apply

10. What practical steps could we take to start sharing our wealth and possessions with one another?

⊡ getting personal

If Jesus said v 21 to you, what would your response be? Is there something else that Jesus could say, which would make *your* face fall? What do you need to do about these things?

Pray and plan for the right response to Jesus' command to follow Him.

⤓ investigate

> **Read Mark 10 v 32-52**

11. Jesus has been talking about the service and sacrifice of the way of the cross. What do James and John ask for?

12. What will James and John experience first?

13. What question does Jesus ask James and John, and what question does He ask Bartimaeus?

14. What point is Mark making by linking these stories together?

⊡ explore more

Look at verses 41-45. What type of leadership does Jesus reject?
What is the model of Christian leadership?
Can Christians learn about leadership from the business world?

⊡ apply

15. In what ways do Christians today seek power and glory without the service, suffering and sacrifice of the cross?

- How can we best encourage one another to deny ourselves prestige or comfort, to live the way of the cross instead?

⊡ getting personal

If a non-Christian was observing you, would they see any similarity
between your life and that of Jesus Christ?
Would a Christian be encouraged by your example to live the way
of the cross? What do you need Jesus to do for you right now?

⊤ pray

Think about God...

• What do these verses show us about the character of God and the
  Lord Jesus Christ, which will help you to give praise and adoration?

Think about yourself...

• In what ways have you acted like the rich young ruler, or like James
  and John? What help do you need to seek from God?

Think about others...

• Think of people you know who are like the Pharisees, the little
  children, the rich young ruler or Bartimaeus. What can you pray for
  each one?

3 Mark 11-12
THE JUDGMENT OF THE KING

⊕ talkabout

1. Can you think of any cases where people were found guilty by the courts, but, looking back, we now see that the truly guilty parties were the regimes that condemned them? Share your suggestions with the group.

⊕ investigate

> **Read Mark 11 v 1-11**

2. Look up **Zechariah 9 v 9-10.** What is the significance of Jesus riding on a donkey?

3. What do the shouts of the crowd tell us about Jesus?

> **Read Mark 11 v 11-25**

The book of Malachi describes the people of Israel complaining that God does not come to sort out injustice (Malachi 2 v 17). Malachi says that the Lord will come to His temple in judgment, 'but,' he asks, 'who can endure the day of his coming?' (Malachi 3 v 1-5). Mark quotes from this passage in Malachi at the beginning of his Gospel (1 v 2). Then, in chapters 11-13, Jesus comes as the Lord to His temple. And He comes to judge.

4. The cursing of the fig tree is an illustration of the cleansing of the temple. How does the fig tree incident help us understand what happened in the temple?

Pilgrims paid a temple tax, but they had to pay it in the temple's own currency. Traders also sold animals for sacrifice. Much of this activity took place in the court of the Gentiles, which was originally intended to be the part of the temple set aside for people from other nations to pray to the Lord. This could no longer happen because the court of the Gentiles had been taken over by a market. Jesus is not simply attacking the commercialism of the temple. He is judging Israel for not bearing the fruit they should have, and for preventing the temple from being what it should have been.

5. What does Jesus say the temple should have been?

Jesus condemns the Jerusalem temple because it failed to be what God intended. The fig tree, which represents Israel, has withered (v 21). But where now can the nations find forgiveness and meet with God? The answer is in Jesus' new community of faith (v 22). Jesus' community is a place of prayer (v 24) and forgiveness (v 25).

⊞ explore more

Jesus quotes from **Jeremiah 7 v 11** and **Isaiah 56 v 7.** Look at these verses in their contexts. What was the false hope of the people to whom Jeremiah spoke **(see 7 v 8-10)**? Who does Isaiah say will be part of God's new community **(see 56 v 6-7)**?

➔ apply

6. In what ways can God's people today, the church, fail to fulfil the role of 'God's temple'? What do we Christians need to do, to enable all nations to find forgiveness and meet with God?

• Come up with some practical suggestions for your group...

...to welcome people from other nations and ethnic groups living in your neighbourhood?

...to offer the welcome of God's kingdom to the nations by supporting mission work?

...to pray for the nations?

⊡ getting personal

What is your own contribution to the work of international mission? How do you compare to the fig tree in these verses? Pray and plan for changes that you can make to your giving, time and prayer life.

⊡ investigate

7. Look at verse 23. The destruction of mountains is an act of judgment. ('This mountain' may be a reference to the temple mount and its coming judgment.) Jesus' community continues His work of judgment. How do our words bring judgment?

> **Read Mark 11 v 27 - 12 v 12**

The parable of the tenants is told 'against' the leaders of Israel (12 v 12). They will not accept the authority of Jesus (11 v 27-33). But Israel's attitude reveals the attitude of all humanity.

8. According to this parable, what is the attitude of humanity to God's Word?

9. What is the climax of humanity's attitude to God in the story...
...and in history?

10. What will God do to rebellious people?

11. What will God do to His Son?

> **Read Mark 12 v 13-44**

12. Chapter 12 describes a series of confrontations. Who initiates the confrontation in each case? What is the issue in each case? Who is judged by whom?

⊕ apply

13. God's people today (the church) must continue Jesus' work of bringing forgiveness and judgment (see 11 v 22-25)? What kind of responses can we expect when we proclaim the words of Jesus?

⊡ explore more

What do verses 13-17 teach us about our attitude to civil authorities? What do verses 18-27 teach us about life after death? What is the insight of the teacher of the law, commended by Jesus, in verses 28-34? What is Jesus' argument in verses 35-37? How can we imitate the example of the widow and avoid the example of the teachers of the law in verses 38-44?

⊕ pray

Think about God...

• These verses show that our sin is so great that, when we get the chance, we will murder our Creator. What should we pray in the light of this truth?

Think about yourself...

• What have we learned about what God wants his people to *be* and *do*? As one of His people, how do you need to pray?

Think about others...

• We have seen the attitude of humanity to God and His Word, and God's response to humanity. In the light of this, pray for non-Christians that you know.

4
Mark 13
THE COMING OF THE KING

⊕ talkabout

1. Discuss an occasion when an important visitor came to your home, office or some other organisation that you are involved with.
   Talk about the preparations that this involved. What would the consequences have been if you were not ready?

⊕ investigate

Chapters 11-12 contain a series of confrontations between Jesus and the religious leaders in Jerusalem. At first it seems Jesus is on trial. But it soon becomes clear that *He* is the judge.

❯ Read Mark 13 v 1-2

2. What is the verdict of Jesus the judge on the religion of the temple?

❯ Read Mark 13 v 3-13

3. In chapter 13 Jesus is answering two questions. What are those questions (see v 4)?

4. What events does Jesus predict in verses 5-13?

5. Look at verse 7. Are these events signs that the temple is about to be destroyed?

6. What comfort does Jesus give to persecuted believers?

> **Read verses 14-23**

Verses 5-13 described events that **are not** signs that the temple is about to be destroyed. Now Jesus describes events that **are** signs that it is about to happen. The prophet Daniel spoke of 'the abomination that causes desolation'—an act of sacrilege in the Jerusalem temple (Daniel 9 v 27, 11 v 31 and 12 v 11). As Daniel had predicted, Antiochus Epiphanes built an altar to Zeus in the temple of Jerusalem in 168 BC and sacrificed pigs on it. Now Jesus says another 'abomination that causes desolation' is coming.

7. What must the believers do when they see the temple being desecrated?

In 66 AD the Jews rebelled against Roman rule. A terrible four-year struggle followed—'the days of distress' described in verse 19. In 70 AD Jerusalem was finally captured by the Romans. About one million Jews were killed or died in famine and the temple was utterly destroyed.

> **Read verses 24-31**

8. When does Jesus say these events will take place?

9. Verses 24-25 quote from Isaiah 13 v 10 and 34 v 4. What do these images describe in Isaiah (see Isaiah 13 v 1 and 34 v 2, 9-11)? What do these images describe in Mark 13?

10. Verses 26-27 refer to Daniel 7 v 13 where the Son of Man comes to heaven to receive authority from God. How will this be seen by the generation to whom Jesus is speaking? (Note: 'angel' can simply mean 'messenger'.)

It is not easy to decide whether verses 24-27 refer to events in the first century AD or to the return of Christ at the end of history. But Jesus says in these verses that they will take place within a generation. Verses 24-25 use images from Isaiah 13 and 34 which refer to the fall of nations within history. Jesus now uses them to speak of the fall of the temple. And verses 26-27 use the language of Daniel 7, which speaks of the Son of Man coming to heaven to receive authority from God. Jesus receives authority to judge and to send His messengers to gather His people through the gospel.

> **Read verses 32-37**

11. Look at the references to when things will happen in verses 5-31. How are they different from verses 32-33?

Jesus has been talking about 'those days' (v 20, 24). But now he talks about 'that day' (v 32). This is the ultimate day of judgment. The judgment of the temple points to God's judgment against all humanity. So Jesus moves on to talk about the coming of the final day of judgment.

⊡ apply

12. During the 'days of distress' it must have seemed like God was not in control of history. What lessons does this chapter give us when we feel God is not in control?

13. What should we learn from God's judgment against the religion of the temple?

14. Jesus applies what He has been saying for us in verses 32-37. How should we prepare for the coming of Christ?

⊡ getting personal

If Jesus were to return tonight would you be ready? Would you found 'on the job' or would you be found 'sleeping'?

⊡ pray

Think about God...
• He is in control of History. So how should we pray about world politics?

Think about yourself...
• If Jesus were to return tonight would you be ready? Would you found 'on the job' or would you be found 'sleeping'?

Think about others...
• God's judgement will be awful. So what should we pray for others?

5 Mark 14
THE BETRAYAL OF THE KING

⊕ talkabout

1. Talk about any incident (from films, soaps, books, public life or from your own personal experience) where someone has been let down by another person. How do you imagine both people would feel?

⊔ investigate

In chapter 14 Mark begins to describe the events leading up to the death of Jesus on the cross. At first sight, the death of Jesus appears tragic and meaningless. But, as Mark tells his story, he shows us something of the true significance of Jesus' death. He also shows us that Jesus is left utterly alone—let down by everyone around Him.

▶ Read Mark 14 v 1-11

2. Why does Jesus praise this woman? What reason does He give?

3. What does Jesus know about His death? What is unusual about the way in which He handles this knowledge?

⊞ explore more

Jesus says, 'the poor you will always have with you'—a quote from
Deuteronomy 15 v 11. Is Jesus saying we should serve Him rather than
the poor? Is Jesus saying it is pointless to help the poor because poverty
will never go away? How does Deuteronomy 15 help us answer these
questions? See also **Acts 4 v 32-34**.

⊡ investigate

❯ Read Mark 14 v 12-31

In the Old Testament, when the people of Israel were slaves in Egypt, God
sent terrible plagues on the Egyptians to force them to free His people.
The last and most terrible plague was the angel of death, who killed every
firstborn child and animal. God told the Israelites to kill a lamb and paint
the blood around the door. Wherever this was done, the angel of death
would 'pass over' that house so that those who lived there escaped
death. The Passover lamb died as a substitute, and the Israelites were
liberated from Egypt. Every year the Jews celebrated this in the Passover
Feast (or Feast of Unleavened Bread).

4.   Mark records the preparations for Jesus' final celebration of the Passover.
As events move towards the death of Jesus, how is Mark showing us that
Jesus is in control?

5.   How does Jesus link the Passover to His approaching death?

6.   What does this link to the Passover show us about the death of Jesus?

⊡ investigate

> **❯ Read Mark 14 v 32-52**

Verse 36 gives a summary of Jesus' prayer in Gethsemane. He fervently wishes to avoid 'the hour' (v 35) and 'this cup' (v 36). In verses 23 and 24 Jesus has explained that the cup of the Passover represents His own blood, 'poured out for many'—His death will save people, just as the killing of the Passover lamb saved the Israelite firstborn sons from death. But also, in the Old Testament, a 'cup' was used as a picture of God's anger and judgment on wickedness (for example, see Isaiah 51 v 17 and 22). Now we also see that Jesus, in His death, will suffer the anger and judgment of God on sin.

7. How does Jesus feel as He approaches the hour when He will personally experience God's anger and judgement on sin?

8. What is the upshot of Jesus' prayer in verse 36? Is it right to describe Jesus as a 'victim' of God's anger? Why/why not?

⊟ apply

9. In this session so far, what have you learned about the death of Jesus?

⊡ getting personal

How well do you understand the teaching of the Bible about the death of Jesus Christ? Would you know how to explain it to others? And how should your heart and life be transformed by Jesus' amazing sacrifice? Pray and think about what you need to do.

⊥ investigate

❯ Read Mark 14 v 53-65

The Jews avoided using the name of God. So, when in verse 62 the high priest asks if Jesus is 'the Son of the Blessed One', he is asking if Jesus is the Son of God—the claim with which Mark began his Gospel (1 v 1). Now that claim is literally on trial. The verdict of the court is 'blasphemy'.

10. How does Jesus say His claim to be the Son of God will be proved?

11. **Read Psalm 110 v 1 and Daniel 7 v 13-14**—passages Jesus refers to in verse 62. How would the religious leaders see what is described here?

⇨ apply

❯ Read Mark 14 v 66-72

12. Jesus tells the disciples to watch and pray so that they will not fall into temptation (v 38). What do the disciples do in the garden? What is the result? Compare the disciples with Jesus. How can we pass the test?

↑ pray

Think about God...
Praise God for the things that you have learned about Jesus' perfect faithfulness, and the plan of Father and Son to save sinners from judgment.

Think about yourself...
Read verse 38. Ask for strength to overcome temptation and to stand up for Jesus. Pray for assurance that, because Jesus was faithful to the end, we will always be part of God's people, even when we let Him down.

Think about others...
Pray for your church, to faithfully teach this fantastic message to the whole world.

6 THE ABANDONED KING

⊕ talkabout

1. Discuss why it is that we sometimes feel that God is not there for us just when we need Him. Perhaps you have had that kind of experience. Is it right or wrong to feel like that?

⊥ investigate

> **Read Mark 15 v 1-15**

2. In chapters 11-13 Mark showed us that Jesus is the Lord coming to judge His temple. What happens to the Judge now?

3. Why is Jesus condemned (there are several answers!)?

> **Read Mark 15 v 16-32**

The first half of Mark's Gospel came to a climax when Peter recognised that Jesus was 'the Christ'—God's promised Saviour King. Mark has shown us the kingly authority of Jesus over nature, spirits, sickness, sin and death.

4. How is the kingship of Jesus 'acknowledged' by the soldiers?

5. Look at verses 29-30. People call on Jesus to come down from the cross and save Himself. What will Jesus do instead?

6. Look at verse 31. The religious leaders say that Jesus saved others, but He cannot save himself. What is the ironic truth in this statement?

7. Look at verse 32. How will Jesus prove He is the promised Christ?

⊡ explore more

It seems that the cross was a vile and tragic disaster, but what view does the New Testament take—**see Acts 4 v 25-28; Colossians 1 v 19-20, 2 v 13-15; 1 Peter 2 v 22-24; Revelation 5 v 9-12,12 v 10-11?**

⊕ apply

8. Some people say that Jesus' death on a cross proves that He cannot be the Son of God. How can we answer that objection?

⊡ **getting personal**

How can it help you through your own personal disasters and tragedies to understand that the cross was part of God's sovereign plan?

⊡ **explore more**

- **Read Mark 8 v 29-34.** When Peter confesses that Jesus is the Christ (God's promised Saviour King), Jesus begins to teach them what kind of a Christ He is. What does it mean for Jesus to be the Christ? Who is behind alternative views of what it means to be the Christ? What does it mean to follow a King who chooses to die for His people?

- **Read Mark 12 v 1-12.** How is the parable lived out in real life?

⊡ **investigate**

> **Read Mark 15 v 33-39**

9. Who had forsaken or rejected Jesus up to this point? What happens in these verses?

10. Why was Jesus forsaken by God (v 34)?

11. What was the significance of the temple curtain being torn from top to bottom (v 38)?

12. Look at verse 39. What is significant about the centurion compared with the religious leaders in verses 31-32.

⤳ apply

13. Look at how New Testament writers use the truth of the cross to comfort, motivate and challenge Christians.

- How can we be certain that God loves us (Romans 5 v 8)?

- What comfort does the cross give to people who feel that God has cursed them and is not there for them? (Galatians 3 v 13)?

- What confidence can we have in the Lord Jesus because of the cross (Hebrews 4 v 14-16)?

- What part does the cross play in our message to the world (1 Corinthians 2 v 1-2)?

- What should Christians do in the light of the achievement of the cross: the way opened to God through the curtain (Hebrews 10 v 19-25)?

pray

Think about God...
• Think about the fact that Jesus was forsaken by God so that we could by united to God. Why not sing a couple of songs that express your gratitude to Him?

Think about yourself...
• **Read Galatians 6 v 14** and ask God to help you live in the light of the cross as Paul did.

Think about others...
• Pray for someone you know who needs the comfort, motivation or challenge of the cross.

7 THE RISEN KING

⊕ talkabout

1. Have there been times when you did not tell people about Jesus because you were afraid or embarrassed? Share a couple of examples with the group. (Don't be self-conscious—all Christians have had this experience!)

⊙ investigate

> **Read Mark 15 v 40-47**

2. Some people say that Jesus simply fainted on the cross or was taken down prematurely. What is the evidence here that Jesus truly died?

⊡ explore more

What do we learn about Joseph of Arimathea? Why is it significant that he is a member of the Sanhedrin Council (see 14 v 53-64)?

> **Read Mark 16 v 1-8**

3. What is the evidence that Jesus truly rose again from the grave?

Other people had risen from the dead (for an example see Mark 5 v 41-42). But the resurrection of Jesus is much more important than anything before or since. It is so significant because, as the young man says, (16 v 5) the One who has risen is the One 'who was crucified' (v 6).

4. Why is it so significant that the crucified One has risen? (Compare what happened in Mark 14 v 61-64 with Romans 1 v 4.)

➔ apply

5. Many people today deny the historical, physical resurrection of Jesus Christ. If we don't believe that it really happened, what does that say about Jesus? And about us?

• How would you help someone who is interested in Jesus but thinks the resurrection is just a fairy tale?

🗩 getting personal

Are you convinced about the resurrection of Jesus Christ for yourself? Do you understand its significance? And could you explain the evidence for the resurrection to a sceptic?

⊕ investigate

6. Why do you think the young man specifically mentions Peter in verse 7?

Most modern translations have a note questioning the reliability of Mark 16 v 9-20. The oldest copies we have of Mark's Gospel do not contain these verses. It seems likely they were a later addition. Some people believe there was a lost ending to Mark's Gospel. The problem is that verse 8 seems an abrupt end. But there are also good reasons to think that Mark intended to end with verse 8.

7. Describe the changing emotions of the women throughout 15 v 40 –16 v 8.

8. Look over **Mark 4 v 35 – 5 v 43.** What are the different ways in which people respond to Jesus?

9. Look at **Mark 4 v 40 and 5 v 36.** What needs to happen if the women are to stop feeling bewildered and afraid?

10. What is the result of the women's fear?

11. What thoughts does Mark want to leave in the minds of his readers?

⊡ explore more

Trace the theme of seeing and not seeing through Mark's Gospel.
**See Mark 4 v 11-12; 8 v 17-26; 10 v 46-52; 15 v 32 and 39;
16 v 7.** Who has eyes, but cannot see? Who is blind, but their eyes are
opened? What is Mark's message for his readers who have not seen
Jesus?

⊡ apply

12. Why does faith in Jesus help us overcome our fears and embarrassment
about telling others the good news?

• What prevents you from having faith in Jesus? What encourages you to
have faith in Him?

⊡ getting personal

What will you do to encourage faith in Jesus, in yourself and others?
Write down one specific way in which you could put your faith into
practice by telling others the good news about Jesus Christ, our amazing
Servant King.

⬆ pray

Think about God...

• Why can you thank and praise God for the resurrection? Share your ideas with the rest of the group, then encourage them by your prayers.

Think about yourself...

• Ask God to give you faith in Jesus—faith that drives away fear. Ask for opportunities in the coming week to tell people about Jesus and ask for the faith to take those opportunities.

Think about others...

• Do you know anyone who is a victim of fear, and stands in need of encouragement to have faith in Jesus? Pray for that person.

The Servant King: Mark 9-16
Leader's Guide

Introduction

Leading a Bible study can be a bit like herding cats—everyone has a different idea of what the passage could be about, and a different line of enquiry that they want to pursue. But a good group leader is more than someone who just referees this kind of discussion. You will want to:

★ **correctly understand** and handle the Bible passage. But also...

★ **encourage and train** the people in your group to do this for themselves. Don't fall into the trap of spoon-feeding people by simply passing on the information in the Leader's Guide. Then...

★ make sure that no Bible study is finished without everyone **knowing how the passage is relevant for them**. What changes do you all need to make in the light of the things you have been learning? And finally...

★ encourage the group to turn all that has been learned and discussed into **prayer**.

Your Bible-study group is unique, and you are likely to know better than anyone the capabilities, backgrounds and circumstances of the people you are leading. That's why we've designed these guides with a number of optional features. If they're a quiet bunch, you might want to spend longer on **talkabout**. If your time is limited you can choose to skip **explore more**, or get people to look at these questions at home. Can't get enough of Bible study? Well, some studies have optional extra homework projects. As leader, you can adapt and select the material to the needs of your particular group.

So what's in the Leader's Guide?

The main thing that this Leader's Guide will help you to do is to understand the major teaching points in the passage you are studying, and how to apply them. As well as guidance on the questions, the Leader's Guide for each session contains the following important sections:

THE BIG IDEA

One key sentence will give you the main point of the session. This is what you should be aiming to have fixed in people' minds as they leave the Bible study. And it's the point you need to head back towards when the discussion goes off at a tangent.

SUMMARY

An overview of the passage, including plenty of useful historical background information.

OPTIONAL EXTRA

Usually this is an introductory activity, that ties in with the main theme of the Bible study, and is designed to 'break the ice' at the beginning of a session. Or it may be a 'homework project' that people can tackle during the week.

So let's take a look at the various features of a Good Book Guide.

⊕ **talkabout**: each session kicks off with a discussion question, based on the group's opinions or experiences. It's designed to get people talking and thinking in a general way about the main subject of the Bible study.

⬇ **investigate**: the first thing that you and your group need to know is what the Bible passage is about, which is the purpose of these questions. But watch out—people may come up with answers based on their experiences or teaching they have heard in the past, without referring to the passage at all. It's amazing how often we can get through a Bible study without actually looking at the Bible! And if you're stuck for an answer the Leader's Guide contains guidance on questions. These are the answers to which you need to direct your group. This information isn't meant to be read out to people—ideally, you want them to discover these answers from the Bible for themselves. Sometimes optional follow-up questions (see ☒ in guidance on questions) are included, to help you help your group get to the answer.

⬆ **explore more**: these questions generally point people to other relevant parts of the Bible. They are useful for helping your group to see how the passage fits into the 'big picture' of the whole Bible. These sections are **OPTIONAL**—only use them if you have time. Remember—it's better to finish in good time having really grasped one big thing from the passage, than to try and cram everything in.

➔ **apply**: we want to encourage you to spend more time working at application—too often, it is simply tacked on at the end. In the **Good Book Guides**, apply sections are mixed in with the investigate sections of the study. We hope that people will realise that application is not just an optional extra, but rather, the whole purpose of studying the Bible. We do Bible study so that our lives can be changed by what we hear from God's Word. If you skip the application, the Bible study hasn't achieved its purpose.

The first part of apply draws out practical lessons that we can all learn from the Bible passage. You can review what has been learned so far, and think about practical differences that this should make in our churches and our lives. The group gets the opportunity to talk about what they personally have learned.

The second part, ⊡ **getting personal,** can be done at home, or you could allocate a few moments of quiet reflection for each person to think about specific changes that they need to make and pray through in their own lives.

Why not have a time for reporting back at the beginning of the following session, so that everyone can be encouraged and challenged by one another to make application a priority?

⬆ **pray**: In Acts 4 v 25-30 the first Christians quoted Psalm 2 as they prayed in response to the persecution of the apostles by the Jewish religious leaders. Today however, it's not as common for Christians to base prayers on the truths of God's Word as it once was. As a result, our prayers tend to be weak, superficial and self-centred rather than bold, visionary and God-centred. The prayer section, divided into thanksgiving, confession and requests, is based on what has been learned from the Bible passage. How different our prayer times would be if we were genuinely responding to what God has said to us through His Word.

Mark 8 v 31 – 9 v 50
THE EXAMPLE OF THE KING

THE BIG IDEA
Jesus is the Servant King who calls His followers to a life of service and sacrifice.

SUMMARY
Mark's Gospel is divided into two halves. In the first half of the Gospel Mark shows us that Jesus is the Christ, God's promised Saviour King. It comes to a climax when Peter confesses that Jesus is the Christ (8 v 29). The second half begins with Jesus telling His disciples that He is the Christ who must suffer and die. The Jews expected the promised Christ to come in glory, triumphing over God's enemies and rescuing His people. And so Peter cannot accept that Jesus must die. But Jesus says that His death is part of God's plan. Moreover, those who follow Him must also live a life of service and sacrifice, modelled on His sacrificial death (8 v 34).

Chapters 9-10 contain teaching on discipleship. This teaching takes place on the way to Jerusalem and is built around three predictions by Jesus about His death (8 v 31; 9 v 30-31 and 10 v 32-34). On the way to the cross Jesus teaches about the way of the cross—the way of suffering, service and sacrifice.

GUIDANCE ON QUESTIONS
1. You could explore whether people think there is a difference between the way Christians ought to view success and the way that we do. To what extent are Christian views of success shaped by the views of the world around us?

2. For Jesus to be the promised Christ means He must suffer and die before being raised again. If Jesus came in glory and triumph then we would all be defeated and judged, for we are all rebels. So first, Jesus comes to take our judgment in our place.

3. Peter thinks the promised Christ should triumph rather than die. Perhaps he hopes to share in the victory. Perhaps he longs for Jesus to get rid of the Romans. Perhaps he longs for Jesus to continue healing and feeding the people.

4. Jesus detects in Peter's words the voice of Satan tempting Him away from the cross. But God's plan ('the things of God', is that Jesus should save sinful people by dying.

5. To follow Jesus means denying yourself, taking up your cross, losing your life and not being ashamed of Jesus and His words (8 v 34-38). The cross has become for us an object of religious art. But in Jesus' day, it was an instrument of torture and disgrace. Taking up your cross means following the example set by Jesus of shame, service and sacrifice.

6. Those who follow Jesus may suffer in this life. They may even be martyred. But they are promised life forever. Jesus will not be ashamed of them when He comes again.

7. Apply: This is an opportunity for people in your group to talk about the ways in which they are sometimes tempted to feel ashamed of being a Christian. Common examples include: doctrines such as judgment and hell, or Jesus being the only way to God; Christian practices such as refraining from sex outside of marriage, or avoiding drunkenness; evangelism in a society where people think 'religion' shouldn't be discussed in public etc.

• How can we be ashamed of Jesus and his words in our evangelism? …behaviour? …and beliefs?
• **evangelism**—we are tempted to keep quiet about our faith; **behaviour**—we end up acting like the people around us in order to fit in; **beliefs**—we ignore truths like judgment because we find them embarrassing.

• It is what happens in the end that counts. Success is being saved (because we lost or gave up our lives for the gospel) and receiving Jesus' commendation when He comes again. This means sacrificing in this life what the world counts as success, and living to serve others instead of our own comfort and interests.

8.

• What has Jesus been saying to the disciples?
• Have they been listening?

The disciples have been refusing to listen to the words of Jesus (8 v 32). The voice from heaven is calling on them to listen to His words about the cross.

EXPLORE MORE

Before God restores all things the promised King must suffer and die (9 v 12). The new Elijah is John the Baptist and he was martyred. The same will happen to the promised Christ. And those who follow Jesus will also experience suffering and rejection.

9.

• What is the problem in verse 19?
• What is the answer suggested by Jesus in verse 23?
• According to Jesus, is it possible for people to have confidence in His words, even when He Himself is absent (see 8 v 38)?
• What do the words of Jesus achieve in 9 v 25-27?

The problem is unbelief and the answer is belief in Jesus. Mark has told us that it is possible to see Jesus with our eyes, and yet still not see Him with the eyes of faith (4 v 11-12; 8 v 21-29). It is also possible to have confidence in Jesus' words even when He is absent (8 v 38).

10. At first sight this verse can appear perplexing. It could be taken to mean that spirits can be exorcised by ways other than prayer, or that some spirits are more powerful than others? However, the main point of Jesus' words is found in the 'prayer' of verse 24. This is the prayer we should pray when we face difficulties and when Jesus seems absent.

11.

- What does it look like when we fail to follow the example of the cross in these areas? (Instead of serving, we might compete with others in the church. Instead of welcoming unimportant people, we might make a point of only welcoming professionals, families or those of our own race. Instead of rejoicing in the work of others, we might envy the success of other churches. Instead of eradicating sin, we might allow ourselves to be in situations of temptation.)

We are to:
- serve one another (v 33-35);
- welcome unimportant people (v 36-37);
- rejoice in the success of others (v 38-41);
- eradicate sin from our lives (v 42-50; see also 1 Peter 4 v 1).

Verse 50: in the Old Testament God made a covenant or contract with Israel. Salt was a sign of faithfulness to a covenant (see Leviticus 2 v 13; Numbers 18 v 19; 2 Chronicles 13 v 5). Adding salt was like signing a contract or shaking hands on it. But Israel had not been faithful to God's covenant. They had lost their saltiness and would be judged by God. The followers of Jesus are now God's new community.

12. Apply: We shouldn't think that we are immune from making the same mistakes as the disciples, but should take the opportunity to learn what frequently causes Christians to fail—in this case, a failure to listen to what Jesus had told them (8 v 32) and a failure to trust and rely on Jesus when He was away from them (9 v 19).

- Get the group to discuss specific, practical measures that will help us to actually listen to God's Word—eg: taking notes from Bible teaching and reviewing them (with someone?) later in the week; talking with others (eg: a prayer partner) about what you are reading / being taught in the Bible, and discussing how to apply it; asking yourself regularly: 'What has God taught me from His Word, and what do I need to do?

- How can we help one another when we face difficulties and Jesus seems absent.
- Again, discuss practical ideas and find out what helps people to turn to God to overcome unbelief.

OPTIONAL EXTRA

How does Paul use the cross to define Christian behaviour...
- towards other Christians (see Romans 15 v 7 and Ephesians 4 v 32 - 5 v 2)?
- with regard to giving (see 2 Corinthians 8 v 9)?
- in marriage (see Ephesians 5 v 25-28)?

Mark 10
THE WAY OF THE KING

THE BIG IDEA

We cannot have glory without accepting the service and sacrifice modelled by Jesus on the cross.

SUMMARY

Chapters 9-10 contain teaching on discipleship. Discipleship is to be shaped by the service and sacrifice modelled by Jesus on the cross. In chapter 10 Jesus applies this principle to marriage. We should not divorce to achieve self-fulfilment. While not denying the challenge of God's Word, you may need to be sensitive to people in your group who have been divorced.

Mark contrasts the way Jesus welcomes children, and the rich man who goes away from Jesus sad. People are included in God's kingdom through His grace, not because of their importance or goodness.

James and John come to Jesus seeking positions of glory and power. They have not understood the way of the cross. Jesus says they must share His suffering before they can share His glory. Mark links this with the following story of blind Bartimaeus, by having Jesus ask identical questions. James and John are blind. They need to 'see' what it means to follow Jesus.

GUIDANCE ON QUESTIONS

1. We are offered instant coffee, instant meals, instant access, instant results and so on. We are offered credit so that we can buy stuff now, without waiting. We complain about internet sites if we do not get information in a few seconds etc.

2.

☑
- According to the Pharisees, what effect did the law of Moses have on divorce? (it made divorce okay)
- According to Jesus, what was the reason for the law of Moses on divorce? (hard hearts that disregard God's intentions)

These Jewish men thought that because Moses made a law about divorce then it is okay to divorce your wife. But Jesus said divorce is not a sign of legal correctness. It is a sign of sin (see Malachi 2 v 16). Moses made a law about divorce, not to encourage it, but to prevent it causing even more harm. 'Hard hearts' is one of the Bible's expressions for rebellion against God.

3. Firstly, it is a man and women who are united, so homosexual relations are not part of God's intention in creation (v 6). Secondly, a man and woman are united in marriage, so sexual relations are to take place in the context of a committed relationship (v 7-8). Thirdly, a man and women are to be united in marriage for life, so divorce is contrary to God's will (v 9). In answer to the question: 'Is it lawful for a man to divorce his wife?' (v 2) comes the answer: 'what God has joined together, let man not separate' (v 9).

4. Then and now, people end marriages with ease because personal fulfilment is what matters to them. If they are not fulfilled then they consider marriage to be expendable. This is not the way of the cross, which is characterised by service and sacrifice.

EXPLORE MORE

• What error is Jesus correcting in Mark 10 v 10-12? (that divorce is okay)

Jesus says that divorce is permissible where there has been adultery. The reason this qualification is absent in Mark 10 may be because Jesus is not advising married couples, but refuting the easy view of divorce behind the question of verse 2.

5. Mark says Jesus is 'indignant'—it is a strong word. The disciples are giving the impression that God has no time for children—that God is only interested in important and religious people. But Jesus shows us that God is welcoming and gracious (see 2 v 13-17).

6.

• How were children viewed in the time of Jesus? What rights did they have?

All sorts of suggestions have been made as to what childlike qualities Jesus commends. Is it childlike faith or youthful innocence or uncorrupted purity? But, by stressing some quality that we must attain, these suggestions completely miss the point. In Jesus' day, children were the least important members of society. They did not count and they had no rights. To receive the kingdom like a child is to recognise that we have no rights and have nothing to contribute. If we think we are important and that we deserve God's blessing then we will not receive it.

7. In those days, in the eyes of the world, it was thought that children were the least likely people to be welcomed by God. The man, however, was rich, and though young, important and religious. He would seem to have been particularly blessed by God, and therefore, an ideal candidate for God's kingdom. This explains the disciples' comment in verse 26. But entering God's kingdom depends on God's grace and God's power (see v 27). Notice too, that Jesus describes the disciples in verse 24 as 'children'.

8. The young man chooses wealth and position in this life and so loses eternal life.

9. Jesus says that Christians not only receive eternal life in the age to come, but also that they are rewarded 'in this present age'. As we share our wealth (and also our love and support) freely with others in the Christian community, so we also benefit from other Christians sharing with us. Notice, too, that we also receive persecutions—this is what the way of the cross involves.

10. Apply: People could offer examples of this kind of sharing that they have seen or heard about in Christian communities both at home and abroad. Suggestions could include both small and large acts of sharing eg: potluck meals, with contributions proportional to prosperity; wealthier Christians (anonymously) subsidising or sponsoring poorer Christians, so that they too can be involved in conferences, missions, holidays and other Christian activities; pooling cars, tools, baby equipment, Christian books etc. so each family doesn't have to buy their own; open homes—eg: a family 'adopting' a single Christian, giving them a spare key and allowing them free use of their home; links with Christians in a less developed country and regular involvement in practical projects to help them etc.

- What arguments are put forward to avoid or lessen the impact of Jesus' words in v 21, and how should we answer them? (In response to v 21 people often argue that Jesus didn't tell everyone to sell everything; that if every Christian gives up all their wealth, there will be no one to support the work of the gospel; that if we give up all our wealth we won't be able to reach most non-Christians in an affluent society like ours; that being rich isn't the problem, but rather, an attitude of clinging to our riches come what may. See **2 Corinthians 8 v 6-8** for the truly Christian attitude to wealth)

- What will help us overcome the temptations of wealth to follow Jesus? (We need to understand that wealth is useless because we cannot save our life with it (8 v 36-37). We need to trust Jesus' promise of treasure in heaven, if we give up wealth to follow Him (10 v 21). This means living by faith, contrary to what we see (with our physical eyes) in the world around us. Faith is strengthened through depending on God, praying to Him, listening to His Word, learning, understanding and teaching the gospel, serving God's people and being encouraged by the godly examples of other Christians. These are the things that will help us overcome the temptations of wealth.)

11. James and John ask for positions of glory and power.

12. Drinking 'the cup I drink' and being baptised with 'the baptism I am baptised with' (v 39) are references to Jesus' suffering and death. James and John must share the sufferings and shame that Jesus will endure. The way of Jesus is the way of suffering followed by glory. We lose our lives before we gain them (8 v 35). James and John want power and glory without the shame, service and sacrifice of the cross.

13. 'What do you want me to do for you?' (v36 and 51). It is exactly the same question (though this is not clear in all English translations). Mark wants us to link these stories together.

14.
- How do James and John view the kingship of Jesus?
- What do they fail to see?
- How does Bartimaeus seek a solution to his blindness?
- How is he able to respond to Jesus?
- What do the disciples need to do about their lack of understanding?
- How will they then be able to respond to Jesus?

James and John want glory without the way of the cross because they do not see what kind of king Jesus is. The blind man answers correctly: he wants to see. Mark is saying that we, too, need to see. We need to see that Jesus is the king who suffers and dies. When Bartimaeus sees, he follows Jesus 'along the road'—the road to the cross.

EXPLORE MORE

Jesus rejects leadership that domineers and controls others. Christian leaders are to serve. Their model is Jesus Himself, who came to serve and give His life for His people. We can still learn from some of the techniques and approaches of the business world. But these approaches must help us serve Christians and enable them to serve God. We should not adopt approaches that help us domineer or manipulate.

15. Apply: This might include things like promising health and wealth in this life, looking for positions of power and prestige, or settling for a comfortable lifestyle.

• Why do Christians fail to follow the example of Jesus' life in self-denial, service and willingness to suffer shame? (We forget that to save our life we must first of all lose it (8 v 35); we don't trust the words of Jesus, that Christians 'receive a hundred times as much in this present age (10 v 30); we are influenced by the pattern of this world (10 v 42) that we see with our physical eyes, rather than the pattern

of the Servant King (10 v 45) that needs to be seen with the eyes of faith.)

• What excuses do we use to justify ourselves? (We think that we are making the gospel more attractive to people, by suggesting that the cost is not all that great. The greatest encouragement is the example of others, so we best encourage others by living the way of the cross ourselves.)

3 Mark 11-12
THE JUDGMENT OF THE KING

THE BIG IDEA
Jesus comes to judge Israel, replacing them with a new community of faith.

SUMMARY
Jesus enters Jerusalem as a king, riding on a donkey as Zechariah prophesied the Christ would do, and being acclaimed by the people as the new King David.
At the beginning of his Gospel, Mark quotes from Malachi 3. In Malachi 3 the prophet Malachi talks about the Lord

coming to His temple in judgment. In Mark 11-12 we see Jesus judging in the temple. He curses a fig tree. Mark puts this story together with an account of Jesus cleansing the temple, so that the fig tree is an illustration of God's judgment against Israel. In a series of confrontations, the Jewish leaders try to condemn Jesus. But each time, they are the ones who are judged. It appears that Jesus is on trial, but He turns out to be the judge.

GUIDANCE ON QUESTIONS

1. An example might be Nelson Mandela and the apartheid regime that condemned him. End the discussion by saying that we are going to find something like this in Mark chapters 11-12.

2. Zechariah promised that the Christ—God's Saviour King—would come riding on a donkey. Mark is reminding us that Jesus is God's King.

3. 'Hosanna' means 'Save'. Verse 10 indicates that the people understood that they were seeing the fulfilment of God's promise to send a king descended from David, who would rule for ever (2 Samuel 7 v 12-13).

4. The people of Israel were to bear fruit for God. But they are fruitless and so God will judge them. They will no longer be His people.

5. The temple should have been 'a house of prayer for all nations' (11 v 17). It should have been the place where the nations could find forgiveness and meet with God.

EXPLORE MORE

Jeremiah 7 v 1-15—in Jeremiah 7 the prophet Jeremiah warned the worshippers in Solomon's temple not to trust in the temple as a sign of their security. God would (and indeed did) come in judgment and destroy the temple. Now the same warning comes to the worshippers in Herod's temple.

Isaiah 56 v 6-8—Isaiah announced that salvation would come to the other nations. If Israel would not bear fruit for God, then people from other nations

would. Now Jesus will start a new community based on faith in Him.

6. Apply: Temple = a house of prayer for all nations. Churches fail to fulfil this role when they do not help people of all nations (either in Britain or abroad) to become God's people—either because they have no contact with people of other nations, or because they only offer them social support, rather than Bible teaching and evangelism.
• Discuss practical ideas that would actually work in your situation.

7. As we proclaim the words of Jesus, in addition to bringing eternal life to some, we may also bring judgment to others. When people reject the word of the gospel that we proclaim, then judgment is passed on them. So our words bring judgment—a judgment as terrifying as the destruction of mountains. 'This mountain' may be a reference to Mount Zion and its coming judgment.

8. The servants sent by the owner of the vineyard represent the prophets of the Old Testament. The people ill-treated them and refused to listen to them. Israel was described in the Old Testament as God's vineyard (Isaiah 5 v 1-7), but Israel did not give God the fruit that was due to Him. They rejected the authority of God and His Word. Romans 1 v 18-19 makes it clear that it is the nature of humans in general (not just the Jews of Jesus' time) to reject God's truth.

9. When the son comes to the tenants they kill him. And this was what would happen a few days after Jesus told this parable—Jesus, the Son of God, was killed. This is the appalling climax of human rebellion against God: when we get the chance, we murder our Creator.

10. The fate of the rebellious tenants in verse 9 is no surprise. The rightness of God's judgment is plain.

11. Jesus quotes from Psalm 118. We are to imagine the builders of the temple rejecting a stone as unsuitable. But in God's purposes, this stone becomes the capstone—that holds everything together. Jesus would be rejected, but God's new temple (the community of people who trust in Jesus) would be built around Him.

12. The key idea is that the religious leaders come to condemn Jesus. But each time He turns the tables on them—they are judged by Him. Eventually they dare not ask Him any more questions (12 v 34).

13. Apply: People are forgiven or judged by God according to how they respond to the gospel—the good news about His Son, Jesus Christ (see John 3 v 18). The church needs to be teaching this message about Jesus, in a way that makes people understand that each one personally must choose either to trust or reject Jesus.

🗹
- People will reject the message of Jesus. This doesn't necessarily mean that Christians have done something wrong in the way they teach and proclaim this message—it is exactly how people responded when God sent His prophets, and then when He sent His Son.
- New Testament writers urge believers to do everything possible to make the teaching about Jesus attractive (eg: 1 Corinthians 9 v 19-22; Titus 2 v 3-10, 1 Peter 3 v 15). Christians can be flexible

about everything, except the message about Jesus that they proclaim, and the righteousness that comes from God, through Jesus. People will be offended by the message, but nevertheless, we are to continue teaching it.

EXPLORE MORE
- v 13-17—'Give to Caesar what is Caesar's...';
- v 18-27—there will be a bodily resurrection of those who have died;
- v 28-34—God doesn't want an outward appearance of respect and repentance, but hearts that love Him and the people He has made;
- v 35-37—Jesus shows that the Christ (whom everyone knows will be a descendant of David), is described by the great King David himself as his Lord (the same word that he used for God), so, while the religious leaders expect a Christ who will be merely a descendant of David, Jesus proves that the Christ will also be God;
- v 38-44—the key thing about the widow is that she devotes everything to God, regardless of whether anyone notices or not, whereas the teachers of the law show public 'devotion' to God only to impress other people and by contrast, have no private, personal commitment to doing what God wants (eg: showing compassion to widows).

OPTIONAL EXTRA
Ask one of the members of the group to come next week ready to share information and prayer pointers for a particular country.

4 Mark 13
THE COMING OF THE KING

THE BIG IDEA
God is in control of history. We should be ready for His coming judgment.

DANGER AREA!
This chapter, like the end of Daniel, and the book of Revelation, is a type of literature know as apocalyptic. It predicts the future using powerful, and sometimes strange, images. One of the features of this kind of writing is that it often refers to more than one event. While the physical fulfilment of much of Mark 13 is in the destruction of Jerusalem and the temple, it can also be legitimately understood as referring in part to God's two other great acts of judgment—on the sin of the world in Jesus on the cross, and His final judgment when Jesus returns. Groups can get bogged down with the details, but in leading this study, try to focus on what we *can* know—Jesus' encouragements to watch, and not worry or be deceived—rather than what we *don't know*.

SUMMARY
If chapters 11-12 are like a trial in which Jesus judges the religion of the temple, then 13 v 1-2 is the verdict. In 70 AD Jerusalem was defeated by the Romans, about one million Jews were killed or died in famine and the temple was destroyed. Jesus warns his followers 'ahead of time'. During the time leading up the fall of Jerusalem a number of people claimed to be the Messiah, but Jesus warns Christians

not to be deceived. The fall of Jerusalem and the destruction of the temple is the immediate judgment spoken of in verses 2-4. But it is also a sign of God's coming judgment against all mankind.

In verses 3-13 Jesus describes events that are *not* signs that the temple is about be destroyed. These events take place 'but the end is still to come' (v 7). The disciples are not to be deceived by these events (v 5). These events are just the beginning (v 8).

Verses 14-23 describe events that *are* signs that the temple is about be destroyed.

Verses 24-31 can refer to one or more of the following:

1. The return of Christ. The events of verses 24-27 take place after the 'distress' described in verses 14-23. This distress is typified by the fall of Jerusalem, but not confined to it. It refers to events throughout the history of the church. Then, accompanied by apocalyptic signs, Christ comes from heaven and the angels gather Christ's people from around the world to share in His glorious reign.

2. The death and resurrection of Christ. Many features of this passage can also be seen as referring to the cross—an interpretation that fits in with the flow of Mark's teaching to this point and afterwards. Jesus' death was a uniquely terrible abomination; and is 'cut short' by the resurrection. For an explanation of this view, see *News of the Hour* by Peter Bolt (Matthias Media).

3. The fall of Jerusalem and the mission of the church. 'Following that distress' in verse 24 refers to the 'distress' mentioned in verse 19— the time running up to the fall of Jerusalem. That distress will come to a climax 'in those days' with the fall of Jerusalem. The language of verses 24-25 is taken from Isaiah 13 v 10 and 34 v 4, where it describes the fall of nations within history. Now that language is applied to the fall of the nation of Israel within history. Verses 26-27 use the language of Daniel 7, where the Son of Man comes to God in heaven to receive authority. So Jesus comes to heaven to receive authority. From heaven He sends out His angels who take the gospel throughout the world (the word 'angel' literally means 'messenger'). The elect are gathered in through the mission of the church as they respond in faith to the gospel. This view makes good sense of verse 30 for the temple was destroyed and the worldwide mission of the church began within a generation of Jesus. This is the view taken in the study.

Verses 32 starts a new section. Up to this point Jesus is telling the disciples when things will happen. Now He talks about events that even He does not know the time of. Up to this point He has spoken of 'those days' (plural). Now He speaks of 'that day' (singular)—the ultimate day of judgment to which all the judgments of history point (including the fall of Jerusalem): the return of Christ. Jesus Himself applies His teaching by telling us to keep watch and be ready—not by speculating about when Jesus might return, but by doing His work. We want to be found 'on the job' when He returns.

GUIDANCE ON QUESTIONS

1. You could play a joke on your group by telling them that an important visitor will be coming to your study... the minister, a bishop, or perhaps a theology professor who is staying with a friend... see if people dress differently, or come extra well-prepared for the study...

2. The religion of the temple will be destroyed. See also 12 v 38-40.

3. See verse 4. The disciples ask (1) when the temple will be destroyed and (2) what signs will there be that the temple is about to be destroyed. It is important to remember that what Jesus says in chapter 13 is an answer to these two questions.

4. False messiahs, wars, rumours of wars, earthquakes and famines, persecution for God's people and the beginnings of mission to the nations.

5. No. In verses 3-13 Jesus describes events that are *not* signs that the temple is about be destroyed. These events take place 'but the end is still to come' (v 7). The disciples are not to be deceived by these events (v 5). These events are just the beginning of the end (v 8).

6. See verses 10, 11 and 13. The Spirit will help us speak when we are under pressure. If we stand firm we will be saved—even through death. And meanwhile, the gospel continues to be preached to the nations. Persecution has often led to the growth of the church.

7. The believers are to flee to the mountains without delay. They are to pray that these events will not take place in winter and they are not to be deceived by false messiahs.

8. The events of verses 24-27 will take place 'in those days' and 'following that distress' (ie: the distress described in verse 19 which was caused by the Jewish rebellion). Verses 24-27 do not describe events at the end of history, but events that will be seen within a generation (v 30).

9. In Isaiah 13 these images describe the downfall of Babylon which took place in 539 BC. Isaiah 34 describes the downfall of the nations and Edom in particular. Jesus uses these images to describe the downfall of Israel and the temple religion.

10. Jesus ascends into heaven where He is given authority by the Father (see Matthew 28 v 18). In Daniel 7 v 13-14 the Son of Man does not come *from* heaven, but *goes to* heaven. He is given authority to judge and the destruction of the temple is a sign of His judgment. And He has authority to send out His messengers to gather His people (see Matthew 28 v 19-20). The word 'angel' literally means 'messenger'. It is used of angels because they are God's messengers, but the word can also mean a human messenger. Christ's elect are gathered through Christian people and churches passing on the message. Many of Jesus' hearers would live to see the beginnings of the church's mission and the fall of Jerusalem.

> ☑ What are the parallels between Mark 13 v 2-27 and Matthew 28 v 8-20? (In both passages Jesus is given authority from the Father. On the basis of that authority, He sends us out to call people to submit to His authority as King.)

11. In verses 5-31 the references to when things will happen are quite specific. Jesus says when things will not happen and when they will. He uses words like 'when ... still to come ... then ... in those days ... following that ... at that time'. He says he has told the disciples 'everything ahead of time' (v 23). But in verses 32-33 the time

is completely unknown—even to Jesus Himself. This suggests verses 32-37 are talking about a different event.

12. Apply: God is in control of history. Sometimes he uses events to judge people and to give them a chance to repent (see Revelation 9 v 20-21). God is guiding history to the day when Christ returns.

13. Apply: The destruction of the temple should not lead to any anti-Semitic feelings, but to fear and humility. The judgment of Jerusalem points to the judgment of all humanity. And so we are to watch for 'that day' by being ready for its coming. We also learn to beware of trusting in religion, rather than in Jesus.

14. Apply: Many people have tried to predict the date of Christ's return. People in almost every era have thought the events of their lifetime were so traumatic that it must be soon. But Jesus is clear: this is a date that no one knows. We don't keep watch by looking into the skies or speculating about when Jesus might return. You could ask: 'What action should the return of Christ not lead to?' We prepare for Christ's coming by doing His work. We want to be found 'on the job' when He returns—not 'sleeping', or star gazing.

OPTIONAL EXTRA
You may have people in your group with differing views on how this chapter should be understood and more generally about the sequence of events surrounding the return of Christ. You could have a debate with two or three people making brief presentations followed by discussion. It would good to end with a focus on verses 32-37 and the need to be ready by serving Christ faithfully—whatever the sequence of events in the future.

5 Mark 14
THE BETRAYAL OF THE KING

THE BIG IDEA
Jesus goes to the cross willingly to rescue His people.

SUMMARY
In chapter 14 Mark begins to describe the events leading up to Jesus' death on the cross. Mark shows us that Jesus is in control of events—He goes to the cross willingly. Jesus knows His death is coming. He is prepared for burial beforehand (v 8). Although He asks the disciples to make preparations for the Passover feast, He is the one who has made the preparations (v 12-16). The Jewish leaders are looking for 'some sly way to arrest Jesus and kill him' (v 1). But Jesus knows their plots (v 18). He freely offers His life for many (v 23-24). The group that come to arrest Him are armed because they fear Him more than He fears them (v 43-49). Jesus' time in the garden of Gethsemane is the ultimate test of His willingness (v 32-42). He sees His coming death in all its horror, for He will endure God's judgment. He asks the Father to find another way. But there is no other way. And so Jesus says: 'not what I will, but what you will' (v 36). Mark also begins to show us the true significance of Jesus' death. His death will be preached as good news (v 9). He is the true Passover Lamb—dying so that His people might escape death, and so that they might be set free from their slavery to sin (v 12, 22-25).

GUIDANCE ON QUESTIONS
1. Personal experiences will give the most accurate insight, but, as the question touches what may be deeply hurtful memories, it has been phrased to allow people to approach the subject indirectly.

2. She has done a 'beautiful thing'. She has shown her love for Jesus in the only way she knows how. Those who criticise her put a price on her actions—300 denarii—but they do not appreciate the value of her love.

3. Jesus says she has prepared Him for His burial. Jesus knows He is going to die and He does not run from His death. He knows He will die in a brutal way that will leave no time for a proper burial. But He also knows that His death will be proclaimed as good news throughout the world.

EXPLORE MORE
In Deuteronomy 15 Moses says there should be no poor among God's people if they live under God's law (v 4-5). But he is realistic enough to realise that this will never be. So the continued presence of the poor leads to an on-going command to be 'openhanded' (v 11). Jesus wants to highlight the extraordinary nature of the moment—they will soon not have Him among them. But God's people still have an obligation to the poor. In Acts 4 v 32-34 Luke's description of the first Christian community reflects Deuteronomy 15.

4. Jesus tells the disciples to make preparations for the Passover Feast, but in reality, He has already made the preparations (v 12-16). It is a picture of the death of Jesus. The death of Jesus is not an accident, but the result of God's preparation. The Jewish leaders are looking for a sly way to arrest him (v 1), but Jesus knows all their plans. He knows who will betray Him (v 17-21).

5. See verse 12. Mark tells us that the time for the sacrifice of the Passover lamb has come. He wants us to see that Jesus is the one to whom the Passover points.
See verses 22-24. Jesus says that the Passover feast is fulfilled in Him. The bread and wine are His body and His blood.

6. Jesus dies 'for many', as did the Passover lamb. The Passover and escape from Egypt point to what Jesus will achieve by His death. Through Jesus, we can escape death and be set free from our slavery to sin.

EXPLORE MORE
God will not only give us His law, but will write it on our hearts. He will enable us to obey Him. We will all know God without the need for mediators like priests and prophets. And God will forgive our sins, so this covenant cannot be broken.
But we are just as unfaithful as the Israelites. Zechariah speaks about a faithful remnant—a third of the people. But ultimately, this remnant comes down to one faithful person—the Lord Jesus Christ. He is faithful to the end (see Mark 14 v 36). The new covenant will last forever because it is made in the name of Jesus, the faithful one. Jesus meets its requirements and, through Him, we too are counted faithful.

7. In Gethsemane Jesus was 'overwhelmed with sorrow to the point of death' (v 34), because He knew that He would suffer (drink the cup of) God's anger and judgment against sin. By taking the place of sinners, Jesus' death would be a 'substitutionary atonement'. When we teach the true significance of Jesus' death, it is vital that people don't get the impression that this was just some clever and painless magic trick to do away with sin. Jesus recoiled from the horror of His death, to the extent that He very nearly felt He would die from the revulsion and stress alone.

8. Jesus ends up praying 'not what I will, but what you will.' People sometimes say we should not talk of Jesus bearing God's anger in our place. They say it makes Jesus a victim of God. But verse 36 shows us that He died willingly, not helplessly. The Father and Son were united. Jesus died because of His love for the Father and for His people.

9. Apply: This is an opportunity to check how well people understand the references to the Passover, the 'cup' of God's wrath and the new covenant promised in Jeremiah, in relation to Jesus' death.

• Some people dislike the idea that God carried out His judgment against wickedness on His own Son. They try to protect God's reputation by teaching that on the cross, Jesus was not being punished for our sin. But why is it bad news for all of us if the Bible's teaching about the significance of Jesus' death is ignored? (If Jesus, when He died on the cross, did not experience, in our place, the anger and judgment of God against sin, then that anger and judgment remain on us. Jesus cannot save us and there is nothing that we can do to escape that judgment. So there is no possibility of forgiveness or eternal life for anyone.)

• How can we answer this kind of false teaching? (We need to show people that this teaching about the death of Jesus can be found throughout the Bible—in the words of Old Testament prophets (see Isaiah 53 v 1-10), in the words of Jesus Himself (see Mark 10 v 45, Mark 15 v 34), and in the words of the apostles Paul (see Romans 5 v 22-26, 2 Corinthians 5 v 21, Galatians 3 v 13), Peter (see 1 Peter 2 v 24, 3 v 18) and John (1 John 4 v 10).)

10. Jesus says that the religious leaders, questioning Him now, will one day see Him seated at the right hand of God and coming on the clouds of heaven.

11. Psalm 110 and Daniel 7 both describe the hostility and conflict of the world

against God. And both passages say that God will vindicate His chosen One. Jesus is saying that this conflict is now focused on His trial, but God will vindicate Him. The divinity of Jesus will be demonstrated through His resurrection, His ascension to glory and His return at the end of history. The religious leaders will see that Jesus is the Son of God, both in a few days' time (when Jesus' body vanishes, they hear the story of the resurrection and ascension, and thousands become Christians), and when Jesus returns to judge the world.

12. Apply: Jesus passes His hour of testing. The disciples also face a time of testing. But they do not watch and pray. Instead they sleep (v 37 and 40). As a result, they fail their time of testing. They end up deserting and denying Jesus (see verses 50, 68 and 70-72).
Focus the discussion on standing by Jesus under pressure.
Encourage people to share their personal experiences. Use the follow-up questions below to tease out application.

• The Disciples failed to stand by Jesus in their time of testing. How are we tested today? (We need to understand that we are just like the disciples—we are not as strong as we like to think we are, and we too would let Jesus down.)
• What do we need to do to prepare for testing? (We need to watch. Get your group to discuss what 'watching' means, and how we can do it. We need to be alert for temptations in the world and in ourselves that will cause us to fail—we need to know and take notice of the warnings and encouragements of God's Word, which can thoroughly

equip us for every good work (2 Timothy 3 v 16). We also need to pray-discuss what we should pray for, and the practicalities of when and how to help one another.)
• How can we pass the test? And what does it mean for the times when we fail? (Look at verse 38. Jesus says that in the face of temptation we should 'watch and pray'. But more importantly, Jesus has passed the test on our behalf. He is faithful to God and we are counted faithful through Him. He makes a new covenant or contract with God through His blood. So even when we fail we are still part of God's people.)

Mark 15 v 1-39
THE ABANDONED KING

THE BIG IDEA
Jesus unites us to God by being forsaken by God.

SUMMARY
Mark has portrayed Jesus as God's promised King and the Judge promised in Malachi 3. But now we see Jesus the Judge condemned—even though He has committed no crime (v 14). And we see Jesus hailed as king, but it is a cruel joke (v 16-20). The religious leaders say they will believe Jesus is the Christ if He comes down from the cross and saves Himself. But for Jesus to be the Christ means He stays on the cross to save His people. Jesus is forsaken by God (v 34). God judges Him. As Jesus dies, the curtain of the temple is torn from top to bottom (v 38). The curtain kept people from the Most Holy Place—the symbol of God's presence in the temple. But now the way to God is open. God judges Jesus instead of judging us so that we can be united with God. Jesus unites us to God by being forsaken by God.

GUIDANCE ON QUESTIONS
2. Mark begins his Gospel with a quote from Malachi 3 v 1-5, which speaks of the Lord coming to judge His temple (Mark 1 v 2). In chapters 11-13 the Jewish leaders try to condemn Jesus, but each time they are the ones who are judged. Jesus is the Judge. But now the Judge is condemned. He is the judged Judge.

3. See verse 14. There is no proper answer when Pilate asks 'What crime has he committed?' except the baying of the crowd. Jesus is innocent. You may want to ask some follow up questions.

• Why is Jesus condemned? (Because of envy [v 10] and fear [v 15])
• What happens in verse 11? (A guilty man goes free while an innocent man is condemned)
• In what way is this a picture of what Jesus' death will accomplish?

4. The soldiers hail Jesus as king, crown Him and bow before Him. But it is all a cruel joke. In chapter 4 Jesus spoke of a hidden kingdom (the parables of the growing seed and the mustard seed—v 26-32). Now we see that He is the hidden King.

5. Jesus stays on the cross in order to save His people. He refuses to save Himself so that He can save us instead.

6. Jesus can save Himself. But He saves others by refusing to save Himself.

7. The religious leaders say they will believe Jesus is the Christ if they see Him coming down from the cross. But Jesus has said the Christ must suffer and die. Jesus proves He is the Christ by staying on the cross. He proves He is the Christ by saving His people.

EXPLORE MORE: First impressions of what happened when Jesus died on the cross are turned upside-down by the teaching of the New Testament.

Acts 4 v 25-28—those who set about killing the Son of God in fact unwittingly fulfil the purposes of God.

Colossians 1 v 19-20—this act of violence is the means by which God makes peace with, and reconciles to Himself, all things.

Colossians 2 v 13-15—the cross (a public spectacle of weakness and humiliation) is the means by which God disarms the powers of evil and makes a public spectacle of them.

1 Peter 2 v 22-24—the death of Jesus on the cross is the means by which we are able to die to our sins, and live for righteousness instead.

Revelation 5 v 9-12—as a result of His shameful death on the cross, Jesus is worthy of all praise and honour, because with His blood He purchased men for God.

Revelation 12 v 10-11—the devil (the accuser of our brothers) has been overcome because of what happened on the cross (the blood of the Lamb).

☒ How do these verses show us God's sovereignty (His absolute power and unalterable control over everything)? For instance, what truths about Jesus were unintentionally proclaimed, during His trial and crucifixion, by Pilate (v 14-15), the soldiers (v 18), the sign on the cross (v 26), the passers-by (v 30), and the religious leaders v 31)?

Pilate: his question (v 14) reveals that Jesus has committed no crime; **the soldiers:** proclaim truth when they mockingly hail Him as king (v 18); **the sign:** what it says is correct (v 26); **the passers-by**: their taunts remind us that Jesus' words (Mark 14 v 58) are about to come true, though not in the way that these people expect (see John 2 v 21); **the religious leaders:** if Jesus is to save His people from sin then He can't save Himself—He must stay on the cross. From this we see that God is utterly in control of every detail of what happens on the cross, and the worst that people can say or do against Him is simply diverted, contrary to their intentions, to His purposes instead.

• How can this understanding of the cross help Christians through their own personal disasters and tragedies? (If God can take the greatest act of evil, the murder of His Saviour King by the very people He came to rescue, and use it for the greatest good, the salvation of the whole world, then we can have confidence and hope that God will do the same thing with the tragedies and disasters that we experience. We suffer for purposes that are unimaginably good.)

8. The Jews could not believe that anyone who had been 'hung on a tree' (or on a cross), and was therefore cursed by God (Deuteronomy 21 v 23), could be the promised Saviour King. Muslims today assert that God cannot die and therefore, Jesus cannot be the Son of God, if, as the New Testament teaches, He was crucified. Throughout this course we have seen that from the moment Jesus' kingship was first recognised (Mark 8 v 29), He began to teach that He must suffer and be killed (v 31), and yet even His followers were unwilling to accept the nature of His kingship: hidden, servant-like, rejected and suffering (v 32). Similarly, those who object that the Son of God cannot die or be cursed by God are unwilling to listen to what God has said on the subject, through the words of Old Testament prophets and the teachings of Jesus

Himself. They prefer to believe in a God of their own imagining rather than the incomparably greater God who has revealed Himself through His Word. (For further helpful reading, see chapter 8 of 'Islam in our backyard' by Tony Payne.)

EXPLORE MORE: Mark 8 v 29-34: Jesus tells the disciples that the Christ must suffer and die, and then rise to life again. Jesus is the king who must die because it is through dying that Jesus saves His people. Peter rebukes Jesus for this talk about suffering and death. Peter wants a king who will conquer. He wants victory without suffering. But Jesus detects in Peter's words the voice of Satan. Those who follow the Servant King must be willing to lose their lives. Their lives must be modelled on the cross-a model of service and sacrifice.

Mark 12 v 1-12: The tenants are the Jewish leaders (v 12), although they represent the attitude of all humanity. We have ignored God's prophets (the servants of the master in the parable). Now God sends His Son to us. But we have killed God's Son by executing Him on the cross. This is the true nature of our sin—when we get the chance we kill our Creator. Make sure people think through how 12 v 10-11 will be fulfilled in real life. God is going take the 'stone' we rejected and make Him the 'capstone' of a new community. Rejected by humanity, Jesus will become the beginning of a new humanity.

9. Jesus had been betrayed with a kiss, abandoned by His friends, denied by Peter, judged by the religious leaders, condemned by the political leaders, mocked by the soldiers and insulted by criminals. But now He was forsaken by His Father. The Father and the Son had been united in love throughout eternity, but now they were separated.

10. Jesus died in our place. He bore our sin and took our judgment. God abandoned Jesus because He was judging Him in our place.

What was the significance of the darkness? (The darkness in verse 33 is a picture of God's judgment. Judgment means being without the light and love of God.)

11. If people are unclear what the curtain represented direct them to Hebrews 9 v 7-15. The curtain in the temple kept people from the Most Holy Place. Only the high priest was allowed to enter the Most Holy Place, only once a year, and only through the shedding of blood. It was a reminder that humanity is separated from God by our sin. But as Jesus died this curtain was torn in two. Now the way to heaven is open. God can be known and He welcomes us. Jesus unites us to God by being forsaken by God.

12. The religious leaders say they will believe in Jesus if they see Him come down from the cross. The centurion believes in Jesus because he sees Him die on the cross. We cannot know exactly what the centurion saw that made him believe. But Mark is reminding us that faith is God's gift. And he is reminding us that God is revealed in the cross. The sign that Jesus is God's promised King is that He dies in our place.

13. Apply: You may want to get into small groups or pairs to answer one question each before sharing together what you have learned.

• **Romans 5 v 8:** many people feel loved

by God if they are experiencing good times and they doubt His love for them in bad times. But God demonstrates His love for us in the completed historical event of the cross, so that, regardless of our personal circumstances, we can look at the cross and be certain that we are loved by God.
• **Galatians 3 v 13**: to be cursed by God means that we can only know His wrath and judgment, not His love and Fatherly care. But Jesus has redeemed us (freed us) by being cursed in our place. Because Jesus was abandoned by God we need never suffer this horrific experience.

Though we may sometimes feel that God is not there for us, the truth is that through Jesus we can turn to Him for help at any time.
• **Hebrews 4 v 14-16**: Jesus has experienced the same feelings (Mark 15 v 34)—He knows what it is like to feel that God is not there for us. But he not only feels with us, He also offers us hope. Jesus has united us with God. The way to heaven is open. There is a better future ahead (Romans 8 v 17-18).
• **1 Corinthians 2 v 1-2**: the cross is the sum total of our message to the world.

Mark 15 v 40 – 16 v 8
THE RISEN KING

THE BIG IDEA
Mark leaves us with a question: will we respond to the death and resurrection of Jesus with fear or faith?

SUMMARY
Mark makes it clear that Jesus truly died and truly rose again. He draws attention to the fact that it is 'one who was crucified' that rose again. Other people have risen from the dead (see 5 v 41-42). But Jesus is the one who was condemned as a blasphemer. Now His resurrection proves He truly was the Son of God. And Jesus is the one who died under God's judgment. Now His resurrection proves that judgment has been dealt with and the way to God is open.

Most modern translations have a note questioning the reliability of Mark 16 v 9-20. The oldest manuscripts we have of

Mark's Gospel do not contain these verses. It seems likely they were a later addition. These additional verses are not in the same style as the rest of the book. They seem to summarise other traditions in the early church. It is easy to see why someone might have added an ending—Mark's ending seems so abrupt. It feels a bit like an anti-climax. Some people believe there was a lost ending to Mark's Gospel—that verses 9-20 replace an original ending that we do not have anymore.

But there are also good reasons to think that Mark intended to end with verse 8. Throughout Mark's Gospel people have responded to Jesus with either fear or faith. Mark ends with the fear of the women who witness the resurrection. Mark leaves us with a question: will we respond to the death and resurrection of Jesus with fear or faith?

GUIDANCE ON QUESTIONS

2. Jesus' death was witnessed (v 40-41). Pilate checked to make sure he was truly dead (v 44). His burial was witnessed and the tomb sealed (v 46-47).

EXPLORE MORE: Joseph risks a lot to bury Jesus. He goes before Pilate 'boldly'. He also sacrifices his standing in society by associating with someone whom his fellow Council members had condemned.
Mark also says Joseph was 'waiting for the kingdom of God'. In other words, he was trusting God's promise of a Saviour King and perhaps recognised Jesus as that King.

3. Women could not be witnesses in a Jewish court of law, but women first witness the resurrection of Jesus, indicating that this is not a story you would make up. The women did not expect Jesus to have risen (v 3 and 8).

☑ Why is it unlikely that the disciples stole the body of Jesus? (because the disciples would not have lived and died for what they knew to be a lie)
• Why is it unlikely that the Romans or the Jews stole the body of Jesus? (Because the authorities would have produced the body when the Christians started preaching)

4. Look at 14 v 61-64. Jesus claimed to be the Son of God, but the Jewish leaders concluded He was blaspheming.
The resurrection proves that Jesus was right—He is God's Son (see Romans 1 v 4). Look at 15 v 31-34. Jesus died under God's judgment in our place.
The resurrection is the proof that He has saved His people. He has born God's judgment in full. God has rescued Him from death, and God will rescue us from death if we trust in Jesus.

☑ How did Jesus say to the religious leaders that He would prove He was the Son of God? (See Mark 14 v 62 and Session 5, question 11)
• Who raised Jesus from death and why? (See Acts 2 v 24-36)

5. Apply: To deny the physical resurrection of Jesus means that Jesus is not the Son of God, and not even a good man, but a blasphemer. It means that we are still under God's judgment for our sin, because Jesus' death cannot save us if He died as a blasphemer.

☑ According to the apostle Paul, what are the implications if Jesus Christ was not raised from the dead? (see 1 Corinthians 15 v 14-19)? And if the resurrection of Christ is true (see v 20-23)? (If Jesus did not rise from the dead then Christian preaching and faith are in vain (v 14), Christians are false witnesses-liars or victims of deception (v 15), Christians are still in their sins (v17), Christians who have already died are lost (v18), and to be a Christian without hope of resurrection in the life to come is the most pitiable condition possible (v 19). But if Jesus did rise from the dead He is just the first, and all Christians, including those who have died, will also be resurrected (v 20-23).
• How would you help someone who is interested in Jesus but thinks the resurrection is just a fairy tale? (Get the group to discuss previous experiences of this kind of conversation. Why not recommend one of the many helpful books on this subject—*Simply Christianity* by John Dickson, *Jesus on trial* by Kel Richards, *The case for Christ* by Lee Strobel)?)

6. Look at 14 v 27-31 and 66-72. Peter had claimed he would stand by Jesus, but three times he denied knowing

Him. He must have wondered if he had blown it forever. So it must have been comforting for Peter to hear that he was included in Jesus' plans.

☑ How would Peter have felt when he heard his name mentioned in this way?
• What lessons are there for us? (Failure need never be final for God's people. Peter's experience shows we can be forgiven when we let God down.)

7. The women watch Jesus die—no doubt with a great deal of sadness (15 v 40-41). They see where His body is laid (15 v 47). The same group of women come to anoint His body (16 v 1), but are 'alarmed' to see the stone rolled away (16 v 4-6). Focus people's attention on how Mark describes their emotions in 16 v 8: 'trembling and bewildered', and 'afraid'.

8. If necessary, point people to 4 v 40 and 41, 5 v 15, 20, 33, 34 and 36. People respond to Jesus with either fear or faith.

9. The women need to believe in Jesus. They need the prayer of 9 v 24: 'I do believe; help me overcome my unbelief!'

10. Because they are afraid, the women do not tell anyone about Jesus.

11. Mark wants us to recognise the need for faith in Jesus to overcome our fears. Mark leaves us with a question: will we respond to the death and resurrection of Jesus with fear or faith?

EXPLORE MORE: We can no longer see Jesus on earth, but we can 'see' Him through the gift of faith. We can recognise Him as our King, our Saviour and our God. God is revealed through the message of the cross.

12. Apply: Try to help people think this question through in relation to the specific fears and challenges they face (relate it back to question one).
•Although Jesus is seen as just a carpenter's son, turned itinerant and homeless teacher, with only a small band of uneducated disciples, with the eye of faith He is seen as the King, the Judge and the Son of God. He has authority over people, sickness, sin, spirits and death. He calls His people to follow the model of the cross, but promises that those who lose their lives will gain them (8 v 34-38).
• This is an opportunity to discuss practical things that we can do to strengthen our own faith and that of others.

OPTIONAL EXTRA

Ask selected members of the group to share something they have learned as you have looked at Mark's Gospel together, and to suggest something that the group could or should do as a result.